ETHICAL
LIVING™

————— ETHICAL —————
# BEAUTY PRODUCTS

A. L. ROWSER

Rosen
YA™
New York

Published in 2020 by The Rosen Publishing Group, Inc.
29 East 21st Street, New York, NY 10010

**Library of Congress Cataloging-in-Publication Data**

Names: Rowser, A. L., author.
Title: Ethical beauty products / A.L. Rowser.
Description: First edition. | New York : Rosen Publishing, 2020.
| Series: Ethical living | Includes bibliographical references and index.
Identifiers: LCCN 2017050839| ISBN 9781508180869 (library bound) | ISBN 9781508180852 (pbk.)
Subjects: LCSH: Cosmetics industry—Moral and ethical aspects—Juvenile literature. | Laboratory animals—Moral and ethical aspects—Juvenile literature. | Animal welfare—Juvenile literature.
Classification: LCC HD9970.5.C672 R69 2019 | DDC 179/.4—dc23
LC record available at https://lccn.loc.gov/2017050839

*Manufactured in the United States of America*

# CONTENTS

The French have a proverb, "*Il faut souffrir pour être belle*," which means, "One must suffer to be beautiful." Perhaps you've heard other versions of this saying in English as well. It's something people often say when they choose to go on a diet or undergo a painful hair removal procedure. But most beauty products don't require much suffering—just time and effort to apply. The worst pain the average person will likely endure is some slight irritation. One reason for this is that the chemicals used in beauty products have been tested to ensure they are safe for human use.

Since the late 1930s, beauty products like makeup and shampoos have been tested on animals like rabbits, guinea pigs, and even dogs. If the finished product is not tested on animals, a concentration of potent chemicals used in the product still might be. It is in these testing laboratories that the real suffering happens—from flesh burns to blindness, lesions, ulcers, convulsions, and death. Even the animals that manage to survive are usually killed afterward for dissection. Since the late 1980s, companies have started moving away from animal testing because of the influence of animal advocacy groups like People for the Ethical Treatment of Animals (PETA) and the development of alternative testing methods, as

Millions of rats like this one die in US laboratories each year.

well as consumers seeking out "cruelty-free" products. Yet these tests still continue today.

Animal rights groups and likeminded consumers also take issue with industrial farming practices and the inhumane treatment of animals like beef and dairy cows, sheep, pigs, poultry, and fish. For this reason, these people don't eat these animals or use any byproducts from this industry. A number of common ingredients come from the remains of commercially farmed animals that are rendered, or cooked down, into oils and fats. For instance, glycerin, gelatin, and collagen are ingredients used in beauty products that often come from this process.

"Beauty is only skin deep," a saying you've also probably heard, means that external beauty is not necessarily an indicator of character. However, science suggests that character influences your perception of other people's external beauty, as well as other people's perception of yours. In a *Scientific American* blog post, the author and researcher Scott Barry Kaufman explores the question, "Is kindness physically attractive?" He discusses a number of studies that point toward the answer being yes. He then ends his post with this beauty tip: "If you want to improve your physical

A doctor eases her patient's concerns with a kind smile and reassuring touch. Researcher Scott Barry Kaufman has theorized that physical beauty can be visibly improved by the content of one's character.

attractiveness, strengthening the content of your character may be the most effective thing you can do."

This is good advice to keep in mind as you become acquainted with the ethics surrounding beauty product choices. As a consumer, you have the power to make choices that will enhance your beauty both inside and out. Each time you purchase a beauty product you send a message to companies about what kind of business practices you will and will not tolerate. Companies must adapt to meet consumer demands. If they don't, they'll go out of business.

## Chapter One

# LEARNING THE LABELS: VEGAN ISN'T CRUELTY FREE

As you likely know, a vegetarian diet includes no meat. However, vegetarians may still eat and use animal products. A vegan diet goes beyond vegetarianism to exclude eggs, dairy, and even honey. Vegans also make other choices in their lives to limit harm done to animals, such as choosing beauty products with no animal ingredients. Many vegans think the farming industry is inhumane because animals suffer when kept in crowded and unsanitary conditions. Yet when companies label products "cruelty free," this doesn't mean that they're vegan. Only the label "vegan" means that a product contains no animal ingredients.

## OTHER REASONS TO GO VEGAN

People sometimes choose veganism for health reasons, such as a concern that antibiotics and growth hormones used on livestock might adversely affect them. According to Harvard Health, studies also

## INSECTS ARE ANIMALS, TOO

Vegans don't use products made with honey, royal jelly (a special honey reserved for the queen bee), or beeswax (what honeycombs are made out of). This is because bee colonies kept for large-scale honey production are often mistreated. While there are conscientious beekeepers out there, at the industrial level the focus is on profit—not the care of the bees. Conscientious beekeepers may take a portion of the honey a hive produces, leaving the rest for the bees over the winter. At the industrial level, bees are killed each winter instead. The honey is then replaced with sugar water for those remaining. Sugar has less nutritional value than honey or the raw nectar that honey is made from.

Vegans also avoid silk, which is produced by boiling silkworms alive in their cocoons. Once boiled, the silk fibers can be unfurled. And yes, silk is also used in beauty products!

Beekeepers open a hive for inspection. The keepers inspect the hive periodically for productivity and potential problems, yet not too often since opening the hive disrupts the colony.

suggest that a vegan or vegetarian diet can lower cholesterol, blood pressure, and body mass, thereby leading to fewer incidents of heart attacks, cancer, and diabetes. While the findings of these studies aren't conclusive, the American Dietetic Association (ADA) released a statement in 2009 that vegan and vegetarian diets are "healthful, nutritionally adequate, and may provide health benefits in the prevention and treatment of certain diseases." However, vegans still have to take care to consume enough essential nutrients like protein, calcium, and iron.

Others choose a vegan lifestyle because they are concerned about the environment. Practices like

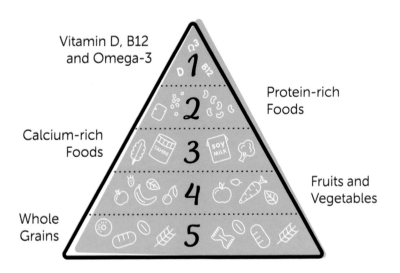

# Vegan Food
## DAILY PLAN

Vitamin D, B12 and Omega-3

Protein-rich Foods

Calcium-rich Foods

Fruits and Vegetables

Whole Grains

In place of a meat and dairy group, vegans focus on getting calcium and protein from plant sources.

clear-cutting rainforests to grow soybeans as cattle feed add to our growing carbon emissions. In an essay in the *Atlantic*, James Hamblin references a study in which researchers discovered that if every American made one simple change—if they switched from eating beef to beans—the United States could still come close to meeting its 2020 greenhouse gas emission goals made under President Barack Obama. That's if no other change was made—only if Americans stopped eating beef.

## WHAT IS "CRUELTY FREE," THEN?

While many vegans do believe in living in a manner that is as cruelty free as possible, the labels "vegan" and "cruelty free" on packaging have different yet very specific meanings. "Cruelty free" indicates that a product has not been tested on animals. Cruelty-free products can still contain animal ingredients such as keratin, beeswax, or processed animal fats.

Vegan products claim to contain no ingredients that come from animals, yet they may include chemicals that have been tested on them. If you want to make sure a product has not been tested on animals and does not include any animal ingredients, look for both a "vegan" and a "cruelty free" label. You can also consult a compiled list. PETA posts lists on its website of companies that are certified cruelty free and vegan as part of its Beauty Without Bunnies program. PETA's philosophy, as the website header reads: "Animals are

NOT TESTED ON ANIMALS

NO ANIMAL INGREDIENTS

The Leaping Bunny logo appears on the product packaging of many cruelty-free brands. The program is known to be reliable in its investigation of animal-testing claims.

not ours to eat, wear, experiment on, use for entertainment, or abuse in any way."

The Leaping Bunny website focuses on certifying brands as cruelty free. The Leaping Bunny program is run by the Coalition for Consumer Information on Cosmetics (CCIC), which is made up of eight animal rights groups from the United States and Canada. The organization doesn't list vegan products; it focuses its resources solely on investigating animal testing claims. There is no fee for companies to take their pledge and sign up, but there is a one-time fee to license the Leaping Bunny logo on product packaging. For this reason, companies may appear on the Leaping Bunny list even if they don't pay to use the logo.

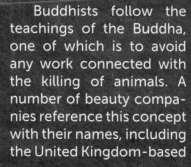

# IT'S MY RELIGION

While veganism is not a religion, some religions are against harming animals. *Ahimsa* is a Sanskrit word often translated as "nonviolence" or "noninjury." This concept is essential to Hinduism, Buddhism, and Jainism—three religions that originated in India thousands of years ago. Ahimsa is inspired by the belief that all living beings contain divine energy; therefore, to hurt another living being also hurts oneself.

In Hinduism, certain animals, like cows and monkeys, are sacred because of their connection to gods. Hindus also believe that people can be reincarnated, or reborn, as animals. For this reason, most Hindus practice vegetarianism. Ayurvedic medicine, a widely practiced type of medicine in India, has roots in early Hinduism as well. Beauty products in this tradition are usually made using plant ingredients such as coconut oil, neem, turmeric, sandalwood, and others. These can be made at home as well.

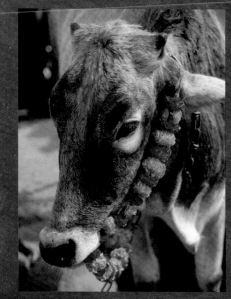

Buddhists follow the teachings of the Buddha, one of which is to avoid any work connected with the killing of animals. A number of beauty companies reference this concept with their names, including the United Kingdom-based

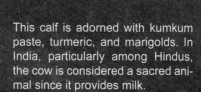

This calf is adorned with kumkum paste, turmeric, and marigolds. In India, particularly among Hindus, the cow is considered a sacred animal since it provides milk.

*(continued on the next page)*

*(continued from the previous page)*

Buddha Beauty Company (certified vegan and cruelty free), Buddha Body Care in Australia (organic and vegan), as well as the more creatively spelled Booda Organics (certified vegan, cruelty free, and organic) in the United States.

Jains take ahimsa to the greatest extreme. They do not eat meat or honey, and some abstain from milk products. They go beyond veganism by not eating certain root vegetables, such as potatoes and onions, because they believe that pulling up these vegetables harms organisms in the soil and kills the plant itself. (When harvesting lettuce or tomatoes, on the other hand, you don't kill the whole plant.) Indian beauty products with the word "Jain" focus on how natural they are. Since India ended animal testing in 2013, all beauty products made there should be cruelty free.

# JUST BECAUSE IT'S VEGAN DOESN'T MAKE IT HEALTHY

A product labeled "vegan" isn't necessarily any better or worse for your health or the environment than any other product. You still have to do your research about chemicals, especially if you live in the United States. In the European Union, more than 1,200 chemicals are banned from use in beauty products because of health concerns. In Canada, close to six hundred chemicals are banned. In the United States, that number goes down to thirty.

The Environmental Working Group (EWG) is a nonprofit group started in 1993 to help protect human health and the environment in the United States. The group claims to have played a pivotal role in Congress passing the Food Quality Protection Act in 1995 because of its research into the health effects of pesticides. The group also runs the Skin Deep Guide to Cosmetics, which is a database you can search to discover where ingredients come from (animal, plant, or both sources). A search also reveals how harmful individual ingredients could potentially be and why. This database can be a helpful resource for getting to know the ingredients in products you're already using. EWG Verified is a program for certifying beauty products that earn a "green" score in the Skin Deep database as healthy and safe. Made Safe is a nonprofit organization doing similar work to EWG. The organization claims to be the first of its kind in America with a goal to eliminate the use of toxic chemicals in everything from household items to personal care. A Made Safe certification involves a rigorous thirteen-step screening process. After the ingredients are run through an extensive toxicant database, they are assessed for risks to our bodies and surrounding ecosystems. Safer ingredient options are suggested to companies if they don't meet certification.

The Soil Association promotes beauty products that aren't harmful for people, animals, or the environment. This group launched the first standards for organic cosmetics in 2002. Along with four other European organizations, the association created the Cosmetic Organic Standard (COSMOS). The COSMOS label certifies that an item has been produced in the most sustainable way, including energy and water usage, as well as waste management.

While the United States Department of Agriculture (USDA) has standards that products must meet to be certified organic, for some smaller brands the process of getting certified might be more hassle than it's worth. On the other side is the issue of green washing, especially for vegan and cruelty-free items. "Green washing" means using language that suggests a product is good for you and the environment when it really isn't. When you see words like "green," "natural," "fresh," "eco," and "earth friendly" on beauty product packaging, make sure to read the ingredients! This type of language can be used on products that contain harsh chemicals. Unlike "vegan," "cruelty free," and "organic," advertisers can use these words without penalty since they don't have clearly defined standards behind them.

Organic and specialty vegan foods often have their own sections in grocery stores. With beauty products, you have to read the packaging and ingredients.

## "UNLESS REQUIRED BY LAW": CHINA'S MANDATORY ANIMAL TESTING

As you can see, there's already a fair amount to consider when choosing beauty products. Yet another issue you'll want to be aware of is China's mandatory testing policy. In order for a beauty product manufactured in another country to be sold in China, the product must undergo animal testing. When a brand claims it does not test on animals "unless required by law," this usually means that the product is being sold in China, and the company has agreed for its product(s) to be tested on animals there.

Some consumers choose to avoid any subsidiary companies of a parent company that has agreed to tests in China. For instance, even though Aveda does not test on animals, these consumers would not buy Aveda products since Aveda is owned by Estée Lauder, a company that submits to testing in China. Other consumers might decide to buy only from the smaller companies that continue to remain cruelty free. For instance, these consumers might buy products from The Body Shop, yet not from the brand's owner, L'Oreal, which has also submitted to testing in China.

Leaping Bunny uses a special icon to signal when a brand is the "cruelty-free subsidiary of a brand that isn't compliant," as this may be acceptable for some vegans; in those situations, the owner or parent company still loses its certification altogether. PETA also acknowledges when a subsidiary brand is cruelty free while also calling out brands that test in China. A page on the PETA website is devoted to highlighting some cruelty-free products you can buy in place of these companies' best sellers.

## Chapter Two

# HOW DID WE GET HERE? ANIMAL TESTING IN THE UNITED STATES

In 1933, Lash Lure, an eyebrow and eyelash dye, caused at least one woman to go blind. Four years later, 105 people died from drinking Elixir Sulfanil-amide, an antibiotic with antifreeze mixed in. After this incident, Congress passed the 1938 Food, Drug, and Cosmetics Act. Now manufacturers would have to provide proof that a product was safe before it could be marketed.

## WHEN HALF DROP DEAD: THE LD50

A drug safety test already in existence was the LD50 toxicity test introduced by the British pharmacologist J. W. Trevan in 1927. This test measures the median lethal dose of a substance. In other words, the test determines the dose that will kill half of the animals, often rats, mice, or dogs. For instance, the LD50 for retinol, a common beauty product ingredient, is 2,000 milligrams when given orally to rats. That means that 2,000 mg is the dose at which half of the rats in the experiment died. Each round of testing done to determine this number requires new test subjects since those that survive are killed and dissected for signs of organ damage. Earlier tests were traditionally carried out with as many as two hundred animals per round.

Some progress has been made since 1985 in devising versions of the LD50 that use fewer animals. One of the tests now preferred is the up and down test, in which one animal is dosed at a time. Computer simulations now make tests more efficient so that fewer animals are sacrificed. Yet the animal test subjects still suffer, the results are still based on how many animals die, and fresh test subjects are still needed for each round of testing.

When the LD50 test or one of the newer variations is administered for beauty products, animals often have a chemical applied to their skin or are exposed to vapor in the air, depending on how the chemical will be used in a specific product. 2015 Environmental Protection Agency (EPA) guidelines for testing indicate that animals can now be "euthanized," which means humanely killed, if they show signs of extreme pain and suffering, such as vocalizations, an inability to move, or convulsions. These animals are then counted among the dead.

## NO MORE TEARS, FOR SOME

Another famous indicator of harmful substances, the Draize eye irritancy test, was invented in 1944 by

United States Food and Drug Administration (FDA) toxicologists John H. Draize and Jacob M. Spines. The test was intended to determine the irritation potential of anything that might come near the human eye, like the allergens in Lash Lure that had caused problems a decade before. Rabbits were chosen for this test because they are docile, have large eyes, and are easy to come by. The original test called for six rabbits each round, but fewer are used now. In 1981, Revlon reported going through approximately two thousand rabbits a year.

Rabbits are placed in restraining stocks in preparation for the Draize eye irritancy test. The stocks ensure the rabbits cannot struggle or wipe their eyes.

To perform the Draize eye test, the bottom portion of the rabbit's eyelid is pulled out, a substance is dropped in, and the eyelids are held shut for at least one second. The second eye is used as a control, or indicator of normal. The substance was originally washed out after twenty-four hours, but in 2002 this time was reduced to one hour. The rabbits are observed for up to twenty-one days for signs of redness, swelling, hemorrhage, discharge, and blindness. In 2012, it was officially recommended that the rabbits be given painkillers, with directions for administering them. Testing guidelines also now state rabbits can be euthanized or otherwise removed from the study before the twenty-one days at signs of extreme pain or irritation.

The Draize skin irritation test also uses rabbits. For this test, the rabbits are shaved, and the chemical is applied to the skin. The rabbits are then observed for a total of three days, or seventy-two hours, for symptoms of irritation like swelling and reddening. This test can also be conducted on guinea pigs and mice.

## ANIMAL ADVOCATES

In 1959, the researchers R. L. Burch and W. M. S. Russell proposed the "Three Rs" of animal testing that would catch on decades later: replacement, reduction, and refinement. They advocated for replacing animals with models or other substitutes, reducing the number of animals used (as in the newer versions of the

LD50), and refining the care animals receive (such as rabbits receiving pain medication).

The Australian philosopher Peter Singer published his influential book *Animal Liberation* in 1975. In the book, Singer reveals unsettling truths of how "factory farms" operate and presents a case against testing products on animals. He also explains "speciesism," which he defines as a prejudice in favor of people and against those of other species. He compares this concept to racism and sexism, then asks: "If possessing a higher degree of intelligence does not entitle one human to use another for his or her own ends, how can it entitle humans to exploit nonhumans?"

Shortly after reading Singer's work, the political activist Henry Spira was given a cat and found himself contemplating "the appropriateness of cuddling one animal while sticking a knife and fork into others." Spira became an advocate for animal rights shortly afterward. In 1980, Spira took out a full-page ad in the *New York Times* that read: "How Many Rabbits Does Revlon Blind for Beauty's Sake?" This ad can be seen as the birth of the campaign to end animal testing in the United States.

Peter Singer also influenced Ingrid Newkirk, the founder and president of PETA. When Newkirk read *Animal Liberation* in 1980 she says it was as if someone had given voice to what she was already thinking. She had worked in animal protection for a decade and had witnessed acts of cruelty so horrific that she would cry as she drove home at night. She knew that there was something deeply wrong with the

*Animal Liberation* author and philosopher Peter Singer is shown here in 2017. He became the Ira W. DeCamp professor of bioethics at Princeton University's Center for Human Values in 1999.

mistreatment of animals, and Singer's book solidified this certainty. That same year, Ingrid Newkirk started PETA with Alex Pacheco, who'd loaned her the book. Gary Libman of the *LA Times* reports that as of 1989, PETA already had approximately 250,000 members.

## BACK TO THE 1800S

The animal rights movement in the United States actually goes all the way back to the 1800s. In 1866, Henry Bergh founded the American Society for the Prevention of Cruelty to Animals (ASPCA). Three years before, while serving as an American diplomat in Russia, Bergh stopped a carriage driver from beating his fallen horse. It was

then and there, as the story goes, that he recognized his calling.

In 1895 the New England Anti-Vivisection Society (NEAVS) formed in reaction to Harvard University's new vivisection lab that was created to keep the university up to date with European methods of study. This

This portrait of Henry Bergh (1811–1888) was engraved around 1850. He remained president of the ASPCA until his death.

was one of the first vivisection labs in the country. A vivisection is a dissection or other experiment performed while the subject is still alive.

The Humane Society of the United States was formed in 1954 since, in the words of Fred Meyers, a founding member, "We know that cruelty, whether to animals or men, creates in the perpetrator a moral and cultural erosion that is harmful to the whole society."

## ALTERNATE METHODS

Henry Spira's advertisement in the *New York Times* spurred Revlon to donate $750,000 toward researching alternate testing methods. Avon and other cosmetics companies followed suit in 1981. However, the years continued on without change. One obstacle researchers faced was finding a substitute for the Draize test. In order to replace the test, they had to replicate its results with a new test. However, the results of the Draize test were flawed, as well as difficult to replicate because of the simple fact that a rabbit eye is not the same as a human eye, among other problems.

As scientists searched for alternatives, groups like PETA continued putting pressure on cosmetic companies. They organized company boycotts and campaigns, such as putting hangers on doorknobs that read "Avon Killing," a play on the company's advertising slogan "Avon Calling." In 1989, a month after this campaign, Avon finally announced an end to animal testing.

By the end of the 1980s, consumers were demanding cruelty-free practices, and a number of companies were meeting this demand. According to a 1989 *New York Times* article by Douglas C. McGill, many in the beauty industry believed that these companies were foolish to end animal testing since it could open them up to lawsuits. Yet the companies were confident that if they combined all the previous data they'd gathered with in vitro methods, they could assure the safety of their products. "In vitro" refers to experiments conducted on cell cultures in test tubes. However, companies were also relying on the testing done by their ingredient suppliers, which animal rights groups still consider problematic.

In 1996, the Coalition for Consumer Information on Cosmetics (CCIC) was formed with its Leaping Bunny certification in the United States and Canada. Two years later, the United Kingdom banned testing for both cosmetics and their ingredients.

In 2000, the Interagency Coordination Committee on the Validation of Alternative Methods (ICCVAM) Authorization Act was signed. The purpose of this law was for US agencies to work together to evaluate and adopt alternate testing methods. Burch and Russell's "Three Rs" was the standard they would follow. Then, in 2013, all of the European Union banned cosmetic testing on animals.

As of 2017, it's illegal to sell cosmetics tested on animals in the European Union, Norway, Israel, India, and

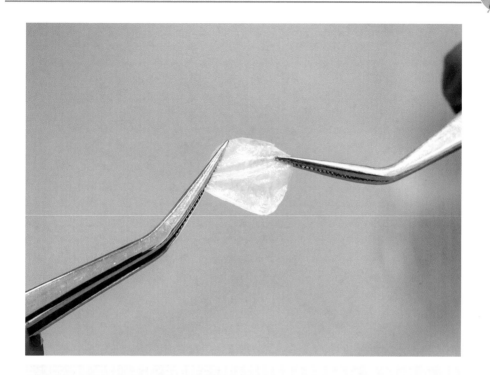

This sample of reconstructed human skin was made at L'Oreal's EpiSkin laboratory in Lyon, France.

Australia. In both Canada and the United States acts have been proposed to follow the lead of these countries. In addition, the number of vegan and cruelty-free cosmetic companies are on the rise. PETA has even been working with China to move away from its animal testing requirement, and the first successful nonanimal test for photosensitivity has been approved there. Meanwhile, L'Oreal has been growing human skin, called EpiSkin, in a petri dish. EpiSkin allows companies to test products on human skin instead of the skin of living animals.

# MYTHS AND FACTS

Myth: If a product isn't tested on animals, it might not be safe for humans.

Fact: Alternate testing methods exist. In addition, the way a rat reacts to a chemical may not be the same way humans react. Because of this, tests conducted on animals can be unreliable.

Myth: It is required by law that beauty products be tested on animals.

Fact: Products sold in the United States or Canada do not need to be tested on animals. In the European Union and other countries, it is illegal to test cosmetics on animals. China is one country in which animal testing is required by law.

Myth: Products with "cruelty free" on the label have not been tested on animals.

Fact: This might be true only for the finished product. Individual ingredients used in the product could still be tested on animals. You may want to double-check a company's claim on the Leaping Bunny or PETA website. You can also call the company yourself or consult the company lists on the beauty blog Logical Harmony.

## Chapter Three

# WHALE VOMIT, BEAVER GLANDS, AND OTHER UNSAVORY INGREDIENTS

The perfume industry may win the award for the most unsavory ingredients in the beauty world. Ambergris is a substance some scientists believe to be whale vomit, while others think it comes out of their other end. Ambergris is still used in some expensive scents to "fix" or hold the scent on the skin longer. Musk from beavers, deer, and civets has also been used. Musk is the strong-smelling oil these animals use to mark their territory and attract mates. As of 2017, some high-end perfumes still use musk from civets and beavers.

A civet is a small, long-bodied mammal somewhat like a cat. Civets are farmed for their musk and kept for their entire lives in tiny cages. Every ten to fifteen days they are forcibly restrained so the thick oil can be scooped out of a gland at the back of their bodies. Beavers and musk deer have also traditionally been killed for their musk. The scent from beavers is called castoreum and comes from the castor gland at

# WINNING THE AMBERGRIS LOTTERY

Ambergris is produced by the sperm whale, presumably to protect its organs from the beaks of the cuttlefish and squid it eats. In about 5 percent of whales, the ambergris sits in the stomach and forms a solid mass instead of being emitted immediately. If you're lucky enough to find one of these rare rocks of ambergris, it can be worth some money.

Ambergris can fluctuate in size, shape, and color. In addition to its use in perfume as a fixative, it has an odor that can vary from musky to sweet.

In 2012, eight-year-old Charlie Naysmith found a one-pound (454-gram) piece of ambergris worth US $63,000 washed up on a beach in the United Kingdom. In 2016, three fishermen from Oman, a country on the Arabian Peninsula, netted a chunk of ambergris weighing 176 pounds (80 kilograms). They were offered almost $3 million.

But because the sperm whale is endangered, your ability to sell your ambergris can depend on where you find it. The United States and Australia don't allow the sale or trade of any endangered animal product so as not to encourage poaching. Some countries get around the act by categorizing ambergris as an excretion, like urine or feces, since it can be harvested without coming near the animal.

the animal's rear. Musk from the deer has not been used in perfumes since 1979, when the animal was hunted to near extinction and became protected. Now, "musk" on a perfume bottle likely refers to the type of scent, not the ingredient. In fact, most perfumes are made with cheaper, synthetic versions of these animal products.

## SKIN DEEP: THE ABSORPTION DEBATE

From perfume to shampoo, creams to powders—most beauty products are going to touch your skin. But how much of this can actually be absorbed into your body? There are those who fear our skin can absorb as much as 60 to 70 percent of what we put on it, yet authorities on the matter suggest that this percentage is far smaller.

Skin is the largest human organ. It protects you from the elements, helps regulate body temperature, excretes waste through sweat, and produces vitamin D from exposure to the sun. Skin can also absorb substances into the body, like birth control medication, some painkillers, and nicotine from a patch. However, your skin does not absorb everything. For instance, your skin will not absorb water. When your fingers prune after a bath it is because the outermost layer of dead skin cells have absorbed it. The oil in your skin keeps the living organ waterproof.

Any substance that makes it into your bloodstream has to go through three layers of skin: the epidermis on top, the dermis in the middle, and the hypodermis that connects your skin to your muscles. Hair follicles, nerve endings, and blood vessels, as well as oil and sweat glands are all located in the dermis. From the dermis, the blood vessels and nerve endings continue into the hypodermis. They connect to the rest of the body from there.

Most beauty products are intended to be absorbed only by the top layer of skin and thereby improve its

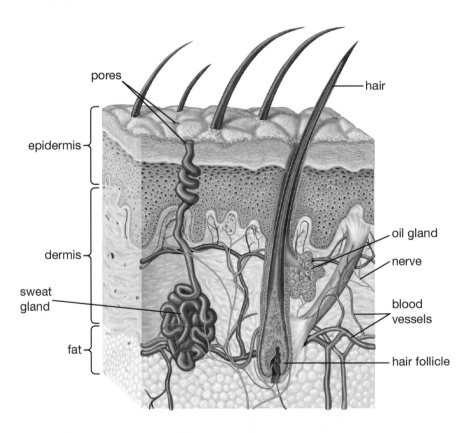

This cross-section of human skin shows how the layers—epidermis, dermis, and hypodermis (or fat)—connect.

appearance. However, some ingredients like ethanol can enhance the absorption properties of other ingredients in ways manufacturers don't intend. The likelihood of absorption also increases when products are applied to the more delicate skin of your face, scalp, or eyelids. Yet some ingredients with larger molecules are simply incapable of being absorbed. To add to these variables, your skin isn't exactly the same as anyone else's, which is why specialists often speak in terms of likelihoods.

## MADE FROM INSECTS

How would you feel about lipstick made from bugs? That's right. Crushed bugs. Carmine is a red dye made from the cochineal bug (not beetle). While the use of this bug is most common in lipstick, it can be used in anything with a red shade, such as eye shadow, blush, and even sunscreen. Petroleum-based red dye no. 40 is one alternative, although it is tested on animals. Another option is annatto, a plant-based dye approved by the FDA. Titanium dioxide can also produce red pigmentation and is only a health concern if used as a spray.

Shellac is produced from the female lac bug for use in nail polish. The female lac bug secretes the substance to protect herself and her eggs. The secretions can be scraped off bark, but larger companies find it easier to boil the bugs. Plant waxes can be used as an alternative, or zein, a protein found in corn.

A farmer collects cochineal bugs for producing carmine. The insects are white on the outside, slightly larger than a flea, and parasitize the cactus on which they live.

Silkworms are often used in beauty products advertised to make your skin silky soft. Yet the proteins in the cocoon fibers aren't effective when hydrolyzed, or broken down small enough to penetrate the skin. It is the other ingredients that do the moisturizing, not the silk at all!

## A FISH SCALE GLIMMER

Some years back, guanine was rumored to be made from bat poop, or guano. Really, guanine is made from fish scales. Guanine is used mostly in nail polish, but it can also be found in other cosmetics. As an alternative, synthetic shiny particles can be used instead.

Another fish product is retinol, a form of vitamin A. It often comes from fish or shark liver oil. According to PETA, vitamin A is listed as "carotene" when it comes from plants. Retinol is commonly used in moisturizers, sunscreen, antiaging products, and acne treatments. A 2012 National Toxicology Program (NTP) study suggested that retinol could speed the development of tumors and lesions on sun-exposed skin. The Environmental Working Group (EWG) urges sunscreen manufacturers to stop adding it to sunscreens, while others insist the findings are inconclusive. Retinol is on Canada's list of prohibited or restricted chemicals.

## FRESH FROM THE SLAUGHTERHOUSE

Animal rights groups like PETA warn against buying beauty products made with animal ingredients since this supports the meat industry. PETA insists animals are treated inhumanely by being crammed into spaces so tiny they cannot even turn around. They are shot full of hormones to grow larger and antibiotics to keep them alive in unsanitary conditions. When the animals are finally taken to slaughter, they are sometimes still conscious when skinned or cut apart. After cuts of meat are taken, the remains of these animals are rendered, or cooked down, to create a number of ingredients used in beauty products.

Tallow is rendered beef fat and is used mainly in soaps and shampoos. Vegetable tallow is available as an alternative. Petroleum-based paraffin can be used instead, but be aware that experts at the EWG link petroleum-based ingredients to health concerns.

Stearic acid and glycerin most often come from tallow, but they can also come from plant sources. Stearic acid goes by a number of synonyms and can be found in numerous products from soap to lotions and deodorants. Glycerin is used to condition and help retain moisture in a number of beauty products including moisturizers, shampoos, toothpastes, and hair dye, and the list goes on. Glycerin was added to Canada's hotlist of restricted or prohibited chemicals in 2009.

Gelatin comes from cows and pigs after their skin, bones, and connective tissues have been boiled down. Gelatin is common in nail polish removers and treatments, as well as other products. Plant-based substitutes include carrageenan, seaweed, pectin from fruit, and soy protein, as well as almond and amla oil.

Collagen comes from the same process as gelatin. Advertisers sometimes promise it can boost your skin's own collagen production, but the molecules are too large to penetrate deep enough in the skin to where collagen is actually formed. Collagen simply works like any other moisturizer.

Keratin comes from horns, hooves, wool, and even feathers. It is used to improve hair and nails. However, you can increase keratin production in your body naturally by making sure you get enough protein in your diet, as well as vitamins A and D. For vegans, protein can come from soy sources, nuts, and legumes. Orange fruits and veggies like carrots, pumpkin, and cantaloupe as well as dark green leafy vegetables like spinach and kale provide vitamin A. Vitamin D can be found in mushrooms and fortified soy or almond milk as well as from exposure to sunlight during the summer months. It's also possible to derive keratin from human hair. Hydrolyzed human hair keratin protein, as this is called, is approved by PETA.

## COULD I GET MAD COW DISEASE FROM MAKEUP?

In December 2003, a cow with bovine spongiform encephalopathy (BSE) was discovered after it was sent to slaughter and rendering in Washington State. After this scare, the FDA launched an inquiry into the possibility of contracting Creutzfeldt-Jakob disease (also known as mad cow disease) from cosmetic products. The FDA report indicates that any risk would be through products such as shaving creams or lotions that might be applied to cut or abraded skin, products like mascara or shampoo that could get into the eye, or lipsticks or balms that could get into the mouth. In 2016, the FDA finalized rules limiting the use of high-risk cow parts, like brain matter and certain parts of the intestine, in cosmetics.

# THE NOT-SO-CUDDLY WOOL INDUSTRY

In late 2015, PETA recorded footage of inhumane treatment of sheep at over thirty different shearing facilities in the United States and Australia. Workers are paid by the amount of wool they harvest, so they shear the sheep as quickly as possible, often cutting the animals and removing chunks of skin. Some sheep are even killed in the process.

A man uses electric shears to remove wool from this sheep, similar to the way in which hair clippers are used on humans. When the blade dulls, there is a greater chance of harming the sheep.

Lanolin is the oil sheep emit through their skin, and it can be gathered from shearing. It works as an emollient for smoothing and softening skin. Lanolin can contain pesticides since sheep are often sprayed, which makes it a potential health concern as well. A company called Sheepish Grins claims their lanolin comes from happy, living sheep, which provides a more ethical lanolin option. A good vegan substitute would be organic coconut oil. You can try other plant-based oils as well.

## Chapter Four

# THE POWER IS YOURS

As of 2017, most scientists support Burch and Russell's "Three Rs" of animal testing. While there is still debate over whether it is necessary to use animals for medical testing and the testing of potentially hazardous chemicals, most people agree that testing beauty products on animals is nonessential. Because of this, shopping for cruelty-free and even vegan products is easier than you might think. Websites like PETA and Leaping Bunny have lists—and even apps—for finding cruelty-free companies. There are a number of popular beauty bloggers and vloggers happy to suggest ethical products as well.

## POPULAR BRANDS YOU MAY NOT HAVE KNOWN ARE CRUELTY FREE

Although L'Oreal and Estée Lauder still submit to testing in China, these companies have bought a number of cruelty-free brands that you've likely heard of and may even use already. L'Oreal owns NYX Cosmetics and Urban Decay. NYX Cosmetics' best-selling products include a powder that works on a range of skin tones and a shadow palette with colors inspired by photo filter effects. NYX can be found online or at Target, Ulta, or your nearest CVS. Urban Decay promotes "beauty with an edge" and has a number of long-lasting products that are also easy to remove. Urban Decay also offers vegan products. Urban Decay products can be purchased in person or online at Macy's, Sephora, or an Urban Decay store.

In 2014, Tarte Cosmetics was bought by Kose, a Japanese brand notorious for animal testing. Tarte itself has stayed committed to remaining cruelty free and offers some vegan products as well. Tarte has kept its original CEO and still promises glamour with good-for-you ingredients. The brand puts a focus on health as well as sustainability by working with cooperatives in areas where ingredients are harvested. Tarte partners with the Sea Turtle Conservancy, gives to charities like Habitat for Humanity, and has initiated a campaign against cyberbullying. According to its website, Tarte believes "in making you feel good inside and out." Tarte products are priced similarly to Urban Decay and can be found on their website, at QVC, or in person at Sephora, JCPenney, and Ulta Beauty.

Estée Lauder has purchased Too Faced and Smashbox, which are both still certified by PETA as cruelty free. Smashbox is born out of the legendary Smashbox photo studios in Los Angeles, and Too

Tarte products such as these have been featured in numerous charity raffles. In 2017, the cruelty-free brand began the #StormofLove campaign to raise funds for hurricane and earthquake victims.

Faced encourages consumers to "own your pretty" with fun options like an eye shadow palette in the shape of a chocolate bar and foundation in a wide range of skin tones. Both brands can be found online or in stores.

Wet n wild and e.l.f. offer inexpensive cruelty-free cosmetics. Wet n wild offers products like nail color, eye shadow, and a contouring palette, all for around five dollars or under. Fans of e.l.f. rave about the quality of the products for the low price, often under ten dollars. Favorites include the blush and bronzing powder, the eyebrow kit, and the eyeliner. Both brands can be found online or at your local drug store.

All seven of these brands are certified cruelty free by PETA, but NYX, wet n wild, and e.l.f. don't display the PETA bunny logo on their website. Also, since none of these brands have gone through the Leaping Bunny certification, they won't appear on that website's list of cruelty-free products.

## INDIE VEGAN AND CRUELTY-FREE BRANDS TO KNOW

The trendy brand Lime Crime offers cosmetics in bright, sparkly colors. They sell "makeup for unicorns," according to the website, for both girls and boys. The brand is certified cruelty free by both PETA and Leaping Bunny. Doe Deere, the founder, confirmed the brand's vegan status in 2012 after products were discovered to contain beeswax and carmine. Lime Crime is active on social media and has a cult following, although some choose to avoid the brand because of a string of scandals. Lime Crime offers many products priced around twenty dollars, with options to buy in bundle. Products can be ordered online or found at select stores internationally.

Sugar Pill was chosen as the official makeup brand for Sanrio's Hello Kitty's thirty-fifth anniversary. Sugar Pill is a cruelty-free brand run by self-proclaimed "animal-loving vegetarians/vegans." Most of their products are vegan as well. Like Lime Crime, Sugar Pill boasts bright, vibrant colors. The products are sold online and in select specialty stores worldwide.

According to PETA, Kat Von D Cosmetics is cruelty free and, as of 2016, committed to going vegan. As of 2017, you can shop for vegan products on the website, although the entire line is not vegan yet. The website features tutorials and an Instagram gallery (#KVDLook). You can find products online or at Sephora or JCPenney. Individual lip color and shadows sell for around twenty dollars, while palettes and sets cost more. Suzi Scheler at the Cruelty-Free Kitty blog cites Kat Von D Cosmetics as her 2016 pick for a high-end cruelty-free brand.

ColourPop is Leaping Bunny approved and offers bold colors like Lime Crime and Sugar Pill. The website boasts luxury formulas priced for experimentation with individual shadows, pencils, and lipsticks selling for around five to eight dollars. The website includes multiple how-to videos for looks like "Iridescent Unicorn" and

Tattoo artist and beauty-line founder Kat Von D is shown here at the 2017 Circle V festival, where she was a speaker. Circle V is a music festival in celebration of veganism.

"Insta Baddie." Colour-Pop products are sold through the website only.

Bite Beauty out of Toronto promotes "beauty for lips that's good enough to eat." The brand is Leaping Bunny approved, and it won awards for its Amuse Bouche lipsticks in 2016 from the Nylon Beauty Hit List and *O, The Oprah Magazine*. Each lipstick is handcrafted for soft, creamy wear and can be purchased from Sephora. 100% Pure is another cruelty-free brand focused on healthy ingredients. The company labels the vegan products on its website, such as its lipsticks colored with fruit extracts.

Charlotte Tilbury (*right*) poses with supermodel Cara Delevingne. Tilbury's cruelty-free cosmetics are popular among celebrities; in turn, she has named some of her makeup after various celebrities, including Cara's sister.

Charlotte Tilbury is a high-end, award-winning brand from the United Kingdom. The company's goal is to "make every woman the most beautiful version of themselves." All products are cruelty free, and quite a few are also vegan but not labeled as such on

# BEAUTY ON A BUDGET: CRUELTY-FREE DUPES

A dupe, in the world of beauty products, refers to a similarly colored product that can be used in place of another. While an internet search will reveal plenty of shade-to-shade comparisons, this is intended as a general guide to cruelty-free dupes that are also budget friendly:

Replace your MAC eye shadows ($16)* with Makeup Geek ($6). (Check the ingredients or the beauty blog Logical Harmony for a list of Makeup Geek's vegan shades.)

Instead of MAC Satin Lipstick ($17), try ColourPop Ultra Matte Liquid Lipstick ($6).

Instead of MAC Powder blush ($23), try NYX Powder blush ($5).

Substitute your NARS blush ($29) for e.l.f. ($3).

In place of Maybelline mascara, try wet n wild MegaVolume Mascara ($3).

Trade in your Estée Lauder concealer wand (or Clinique, La Mer, Origin, or any of this parent brand's subsidiaries that still test on animals) for NYX Cosmetics HD Photogenic Concealer Wand ($5).

Switch out O.P.I. nail polish ($10) for Pacifica 7 Free ($9).

If you like Revlon, similar drugstore brands include Milani, Sonia Kashuk, as well as Marcelle, which is sold mainly in stores in Canada and is also dermatologist approved.

If you like Benefit, try the Balm instead.

If you like the bright colors and the longer hold of theatrical-quality makeup, you can trade in Makeup Forever's eye shadow ($21) for Obsessive Compulsive Cosmetics Loose Color Concentrates ($15, vegan, and cruelty free).

If Victoria's Secret makes your go-to scent, try something new from Bath and Body Works or Twinkle Apothecary ($15) online. Consult PETA's website for a longer list of fragrances.

*Keep in mind that in different stores and during different times of the year, the prices of any product may vary. However, this list is intended to give a general idea of how much money can be saved by switching from popular cosmetic brands to cruelty-free alternatives.

the website. You can go to the beauty blog Logical Harmony to find a complete list of the brand's vegan items. Unless you're visiting the United Kingdom, you'll have to buy Charlotte Tilbury products online.

## VEGAN BEAUTY VLOGGERS TO FOLLOW

Carli Bybel hosts a popular YouTube channel out of New Jersey with over five million subscribers, as well as a website. Bybel's channel features makeup tutorials and cruelty-free product hauls. She went vegan in April 2016 and vlogs about her decision. In 2017, she launched her own product line, Pranava Beauty, which she claims is vegan and cruelty free.

LaMadelynn is a YouTube vlogger passionate about veganism, French cinema, and sustainable fashion.

Popular beauty vlogger Carli Bybel, seen here attending a show at the New York Fashion Week, chose to pursue a vegan lifestyle in 2016.

Her makeup tutorials aren't always limited to cruelty-free and vegan products, but she makes sure to highlight them.

Kiera Rose is a British vlogger with a pet rat, Louie. She does segments on beauty product hauls, trying out vegan cosmetic brands like Lush. She also makes videos on topics such as tattoos, hair, mental health, and cosplay. Her channel even features Q&As, including one about veganism.

Jasmine Rose is based in New York and vlogs mostly about hair and makeup. She does makeup tutorials, as well as reviews and color swatch demonstrations specific to dark skin. She went vegan in February 2016.

Tashina Combs is based in California. Her YouTube channel is an extension of the blog Logical Harmony, which includes weekly updated lists of cruelty-free and vegan products. The website lists vegan items for brands like Kylie's Cosmetics that don't label vegan

Vegan vloggers don't just create makeup tutorials to help viewers learn how to apply products—they can also be useful for finding new cruelty-free brands and items to try.

products themselves. Logical Harmony also provides helpful cruelty-free shopping guides specific to Target, Sephora, and Ulta. In her YouTube videos, Combs demonstrates color swatches and unboxes products to share with viewers. New videos are uploaded regularly.

Another blog to check out is Cruelty-Free Kitty run by Suzi Scheler. Cruelty-Free Kitty includes shopping guides and cruelty-free lists based on PETA and Leaping Bunny certifications, as well as product ratings and dupes.

# 10 GREAT QUESTIONS TO ASK A VEGAN

1.  What made you decide to become a vegan?

2.  Are vegan cosmetics usually more expensive?

3.  Can I find vegan beauty products at a drugstore?

4.  How can I tell if a product is vegan if it isn't labeled? Are there key ingredients I can look for?

5.  How can I be sure a product or its individual ingredients weren't tested on animals?

6.  Can I still be vegan if I use lip balm with beeswax in it?

7.  If an ingredient could come from a plant or an animal, how can I tell which source is used?

8.  Where can I find products that are vegan and also use natural ingredients?

9.  What does it mean if a product is certified cruelty free on the PETA website but not Leaping Bunny or the other way around?

10. Do you believe in buying products from cruelty-free brands that are owned by larger companies that test on animals? Why or why not?

# GLOSSARY

**absorption** With regards to skin, to make it through all three layers and into the bloodstream; the penetration of a product or chemical into the skin.

**allergen** A substance that causes an allergic reaction.

**by-product** Products that can be made from the discards of an original product or its leftovers.

**conscientious** Making an effort to do what is right.

**cruelty free** A label used to designate products that have not been tested on animals.

**dermatologist** One who studies the skin and ailments specific to it.

**ethical** Referring to a greater societal understanding.

**excretion** Something that is voided from the body.

**extract** A condensed version of a substance.

**fortified** When vitamins or minerals are added to a product; enriched.

**hydrolyzed** Containing fats that were broken down in an alkali (opposite of acidic) substance.

**inconclusive** An outcome that is not clear.

**industrial** A business model that puts cost-saving measures and profit first.

**inhumane** Without mercy or compassion for others.

**molecule** A number of atoms bonded together.

**organic** Grown without synthetic preservatives, petrochemicals, ionizing radiation, or any other methods deemed inorganic.

**petroleum based**  Ingredients made from petroleum, or crude oil, which is what is used to make gasoline and other fuels, such as mineral oil, paraffin, and petroleum jelly.

**pharmacologist**  Someone who practices pharmacology, the study of medicinal drugs.

**pigment**  Color.

**potentially**  When an outcome is not certain, yet evidence suggests it could happen.

**subsidiary**  A smaller company owned by a larger parent company.

**sustainability**  Responsibly harvesting, using, and replenishing resources so as not to deplete them.

**synthetic**  When something is made with chemicals to simulate something that occurs naturally.

**toxicologist**  Someone who studies toxicology, the study of poisons.

**vegan**  A philosophy that includes eating no animal products, wearing no products made from animals (such as leather and wool), using no beauty or household products that include animal ingredients, and not attending events like horseraces or circuses that have been known to abuse animals.

# FOR MORE INFORMATION

Animal Justice
5700-100 King Street West
Toronto, ON M5X 1C7
Canada
Website: https://www.animaljustice.ca
Facebook: @animaljusticecanada
Twitter: @AnimalJustice
Instagram: @animaljustice_
Animal Justice fights for animal rights in Canada. The
    website includes a blog and a searchable animal
    justice law library.

Canadian Council on Animal Care (CCAC)
190 O'Connor Street, Suite 800
Ottowa, ON K2P 2R3
Canada
(613) 238-4031
Website: https://www.ccac.ca
The CCAC sets the standards for animal testing in
    Canada and makes sure the standards are im-
    plemented consistently and appropriately nation-
    wide. The website provides information on how
    animal-based science is conducted in Canada.

Canadians for the Ethical Treatment of Farmed Ani-
    mals (CETFA)
PO Box 18024

Vancouver, BC V6M 4L3
Canada
Website: https://www.cetfa.org
Facebook: @CETFA.News
CETFA attempts to raise awareness about the treatment of farm animals in Canada, help people make
ethical food choices, and encourage people to join
campaigns to take action. They offer information
about current animal rights issues.

Coalition for Consumer Information on Cosmetics
(CCIC)
PO Box 56537
Philadelphia, PA 19111
(888) 546-2242
Website: www.leapingbunny.org
Facebook: @leapingbunny
Twitter: @LeapingBunny
The Leaping Bunny website run by the CCIC offers
lists of brands the CCIC has certified cruelty free,
as well as an app you can download. Companies
pay to use the Leaping Bunny logo but may be
listed for free.

Environmental Working Group (EWG)
1436 U Street NW, Suite 100
Washington, DC 20009
(202) 667-6982
Website: www.ewg.org
Facebook: @ewg.org

Twitter: @ewg
Instagram: @environmentalworkinggroup
The EWG offers a variety of consumer guides, including the Skin Deep Guide to Cosmetics. Type ingredients from your beauty products into this searchable database to find out about potential health risks as well as where the ingredients come from.

Humane Society of Canada (HSC)
409-120 Carlton Street
Toronto, ON M5A 4K2
Canada
(800) 641-5463
Website: https://www.humanesociety.com
Facebook: @TheHumaneSocietyofCanada
Twitter: @HSCanada
HSC believes in protecting animals and the earth. The website links to articles about climate change, veganism, disaster relief, and pet recovery.

Humane Society of the United States (HSUS)
1255 23rd Street NW, Suite 450
Washington, DC 20037
(202) 452-1100
Website: www.humanesociety.org
Facebook: @humanesociety
Twitter: @HumaneSociety
The HSUS shares news about animal rights issues, cosmetics testing, and disaster relief. They also include information specific to each state.

People for the Ethical Treatment of Animals (PETA)
510 Front Street
Norfolk, VA 23510
(757) 622-PETA
Website: https://www.peta.org
Facebook: @official.peta
Twitter: @peta
PETA offers a wealth of information about animal
    rights issues and the animal advocates working
    on their behalf. The website offers lists of product
    ingredients that come from animals as well as lists
    of cruelty-free and vegan cosmetics.

US Food and Drug Administration (FDA)
10903 New Hampshire Avenue
Silver Spring, MD 20993
(888) 463-6332
Website: https://www.fda.gov
Facebook: @FDA
Twitter: @US_FDA
The FDA provides information about cosmetic product
    ingredients, related research, required labeling,
    and other news and guidelines.

# FOR FURTHER READING

Bennett, Beverly Lynn, and Ray Sammartano. *The Complete Idiot's Guide to Vegan Living.* New York, NY: Alpha, 2012.

Brunner, Kym. *Flip the Bird.* New York, NY: Houghton Mifflin Harcourt, 2016.

Davis, Janet M. *The Gospel of Kindness: Animal Welfare and the Making of Modern America.* Oxford, UK: Oxford UP, 2016.

Elliott, Melisser. *The Vegan Girl's Guide to Life: Cruelty-Free Crafts, Recipes, Beauty Secrets and More.* New York, NY: Skyhorse Publishing, Inc., 2010.

Evans, Kimberly Masters. *Animal Rights.* Farmington Hills, MI: Gale Cengage Learning, 2016.

Gottfried, Maya. *Vegan Love: Dating and Partnering for the Cruelty-Free Gal, with Fashion, Makeup & Wedding Tips.* New York, NY: Skyhorse Publishing, 2017.

Hasan, Heather. *Meat: From the Farm to Your Table (The Truth About the Food Supply).* New York, NY: Rosen Central, 2013.

Mello, Deborah Fletcher. *Sweet Stallion.* Ontario, Canada: Harlequin Kimani, 2017.

Subramanian, Sunny. *The Compassionate Chick's Guide to DIY Beauty: 125 Recipes for Vegan, Gluten-Free, Cruelty-Free Makeup, Skin & Hair Products.* Toronto, Canada: Robert Rose, 2016.

Visak, Tatjana, and Robert Garner. *The Ethics of Killing Animals.* Oxford, UK: Oxford UP, 2016.

Bekhechi, Mimi. "A Wool Jumper Is Just as Cruel as a Mink Coat." *Independent*, July 16, 2014. http://www.independent.co.uk/voices/comment/a-wool-jumper-is-just-as-cruel-as-a-mink-coat-9610133.html.

Bennett, James. "Lash Lure." Cosmetics and Skin, August 3, 2015. http://www.cosmeticsandskin.com/bcb/lash-lure.php.

Canadian Council on Animal Care. "Three Rs." Three Rs Microsite. Retrieved September 14, 2017. http://3rs.ccac.ca/en/about/three-rs.html.

Center for Food Safety and Applied Nutrition. "Potential Contaminants—An Evaluation of the Risk of Variant Creutzfeldt-Jakob Disease from Exposure to Cattle-Derived Protein Used in Cosmetics." US Food and Drug Administration, July 27, 2015. https://www.fda.gov/Cosmetics/ProductsIngredients/PotentialContaminants/ucm137012.htm.

Dallmeier, Lorraine. "Can Cosmetics be Absorbed into Your Bloodstream?" Herb & Hedgerow. Retrieved September 22, 2017. http://www.herbhedgerow.co.uk/can-cosmetics-be-absorbed-into-your-bloodstream.

Elliott, Annabel Fenwick. "The Cruelty-Free Cosmetics Con: The Top Make-Up Brands Testing on Animals Abroad (And the Ones You CAN Trust)." *Daily Mail*, August 20, 2015. http://www.dailymail.co.uk/femail/article-3127995/The-cruelty-free-cosmetics-make

-brands-testing-animals-abroad-ones-trust.html.

EWG. "EWG's Skin Deep Cosmetics Database." Retrieved September 5, 2017. https://www.ewg.org /skindeep.

Goodwin, Michael. "The Easing of Creaturely Pain." *New York Times*, March 1, 1981. https://www.nytimes .com/1981/03/01/weekinreview/the-easing-of -creaturely-pain.html.

Hamblin, James. "If Everyone Ate Beans Instead of Beef." *Atlantic*, August 2, 2017. https://www.theatlantic.com/health/archive/2017/08 /if-everyone-ate-beans-instead-of-beef/535536.

Harvard Health Publishing. "Becoming a Vegetarian." March 18, 2016. https://www.health.harvard.edu /staying-healthy/becoming-a-vegetarian.

Kaufman, Scott Barry. "Is Kindness Physically Attractive?" *Scientific American*, October 9, 2014. https://blogs.scientificamerican.com/beautiful-minds /is-kindness-physically-attractive.

Libman, Gary. "On the Cutting Edge of Animal Rights Activism." *Los Angeles Times*, April 28, 1989. http:// articles.latimes.com/1989-04-28/news/vw-1780_1 _animal-rights-group-peta-s-campaign-avon -products.

Locklear, Mallory. "5 Icky Animal Odors That Are Prized by Perfumers." *Discover*, October 13, 2014. http://discovermagazine.com/2014/oct/0-animal -odors-perfume.

McGill, Douglas C. "Cosmetics Companies Quietly Ending Animal Tests." *New York Times*, August 2, 1989.

http://www.nytimes.com/1989/08/02/business
/cosmetics-companies-quietly-ending-animal
-tests.html.

Moran, Jim. "Beauty and the Beasts: The U.S. Should Ban Testing Cosmetics on Animals." *Scientific American*, May 28, 2014. https://www.scientificamerican.com/article/beauty-and-the-beasts-the-u-s-should-ban-testing-cosmetics-on-animals.

Prinsen, Menk K., Coenraad F. M. Hendriksen, Cyrille A. M. Krul, and Ruud A. Woutersen. "The Isolated Chicken Eye Test to Replace the Draize Test in Rabbits." Science Direct, February 10, 2017. http://www.sciencedirect.com/science/article/pii/S0273230017300090.

Romanowksi, Perry, and Randy Schueller. "The Truth about Silk and Cashmere Proteins." The Beauty Brains. Retrieved September 22, 2017. http://thebeautybrains.com/2007/01/the-truth-about-silk-and-cashmere-proteins.

Tremblay, Sylvie. "Nutrients Affecting Keratin Production." SF Gate. Retrieved September 22, 2017. http://healthyeating.sfgate.com/nutrients-affecting-keratin-production-10393.html.

Yoquinto, Luke. "The Truth About Red Food Dye Made from Bugs." Live Science, April 27, 2012. https://www.livescience.com/36292-red-food-dye-bugs-cochineal-carmine.html.

# INDEX

# ABOUT THE AUTHOR

A. L. Rowser grew up with a love for animals and currently houses three cats. She has been a vegetarian by preference since very young and by practice once she was old enough to determine her own diet. She has friends and family members who are committed vegans and was already conscious of using cruelty-free products. However, doing research for this book opened her eyes to the animal ingredients used in even basic staples like shampoo and lip gloss. She plans to buy vegan beauty products from now on.

# PHOTO CREDITS